"Thomas's language is carefully crafted, fresh, surprising and often startling, sometimes with a rye humor and deep, deep empathy most often for the world's creatures. Her insight is laser focused, serving up heart-felt truths in brilliant prose about the inhabitants of this endangered world, whether her own chicken-hunting dog from her childhood or frogs or bears or eagles or the cacti of the Southwest…There is always a revelation to be found at the end of her poems, a compassionate zinger I look forward to, a summing up of what is most important…and always it is about how precious and perilous life can be."

—J.Carter Merwin, artist and author of thirteen books for adults, young adults, and children and publisher at MacGregor House

"The poems in this collection offer an unflinching look at the human capacity for cruelty, particularly toward animals. At the same time, the poems reveal an empathic connection and radiate compassion for many things in this world, especially living things. Poem after poem captures the reader, holding you in the grip of language, then releases you, sometimes gently, occasionally roughly, but always changed from the experience… These meticulously crafted poems offer much to appreciate in terms of structure, sound elements, imagery, and meaning… There is music in the language, descriptions are crisp as a November day, and the imagery is transcendently sublime."

—David Mook, MFA, author of Each Leaf

"Joyce Thomas uses irony and humor to alert us to human frailty and environmental desecration. Whether it's a Mesozoic footprint, an osprey atop a communication tower, or a mastodon preserved forever in the La Brea Tar Pits, her images are unforgettable. These poems will help us to carry on in uncertain times."

—George Longenecker, author of *Star Route* and past president of the Poetry Society of Vermont

Some Things in This World

Some Things In This World ©2024 Joyce Thomas
Release Date: March 4, 2025
All Rights Reserved.

Printed in the USA. First printing.

Published by Rootstock Publishing
an imprint of Ziggy Media LLC
Montpelier, Vermont 05602
info@rootstockpublishing.com
www.rootstockpublishing.com

Softcover ISBN: 978-1-57869-186-9
Library of Congress Number: TBD

Book design by Eddie Vincent, ENC Graphic Services.
Cover Photo: Red-eyed tree frog in the rainforest of Costa Rica by Harry Collins Photography, Shutterstock.

No part of this book may be reproduced or transmitted in any form or by any means whatsoever without express written permission from the publisher, except in the case of brief quotations embodied in critical articles and reviews. For reprint permission, email info@rootstockpublishing.com.

To schedule a reading, contact the author at thomasaug@comcast.net.

Some Things in This World

poems by
Joyce Thomas

Rootstock Publishing

Montpelier, VT

ACKNOWLEDGMENTS

"Driving through the Reservation," in WOMR Poetry Contest third place winner, *Provincetown Magazine* VOL. 42.01, April 2019.

"Mary," in *Washing Birds,* Main Street Rag, 2016.

"Aquarium," in *The Mountain Troubadour*, VOL LXV, Poetry Society of Vermont, 2019.

"In Praise of Three-legged Dogs," in *Skins*, Fithian Press, 2001.

"November," in *The Mountain Troubadour*, VOL LXVI, Poetry Society of Vermont, 2020.

"Visitation," in *Birchsong: Poetry Centered in Vermont,* VOL II, eds. Gilborn, Cone, Mook, et. al., The Blueline Press, 2018.

"... despite dumps, mopes, Mondays, sheets like dirty plates, tomorrow falling toward you like a tower ... you do against the odds what Demosthenes did by the Aegean: shape pebbles into syllables and make stones sound..."

—*William H. Gass, On Being Blue:*
A Philosophical Inquiry

Table of Contents

In Praise of Three-Legged Dogs 1
My Friend Said 2
Dead Frogs 3
Driving Through the Reservation 5
Impressions 6
The Joshua Trees 8
Saguaro Reverie 10
Hey Diddle 11
Another Dog Story 12
Free Range 13
The Ladies in Their Hats 14
Fake Birds 16
To Neuter, or Not 19
Falling Iguanas 20
Like the Cheese, the Camel 22
La Brea Tar Pits 24
Where Balloons Go 26
Think of Penguins 27
Champlain Polar Bears 29
Storm Warnings 31
Used to Be 33
What I Remember: 34
Mary 35
Frost: 37
My Neighbor's Pigs 38
Doesn't Much Matter 40
No Poetry Lies 43
1968 45

The Dog in *Life*	47
Synchronicity	49
Visitation	52
Speaking of Fat Bear Week, Katmai, Alaska	53
November	55
Ode: Ice Grips	56
Off-Hours at the Launderette	57
Aquarium	59
Sometimes the Trees	60
What Remains	61
Some Things in This World	62
Notes	64
About the Author	65

In Praise of Three-Legged Dogs

Mostly, you see them in the country,
the solitary mongrel walking not quite right

down one-lane gravel or guarding from its stoop a trailer;
the black-and-tan mix lying in a spot of sun

beside the lone gas pump just where you
want to pull in, and when he at last

gets up, you see how one thigh simply ends
incomplete, in air.

Like warriors they often boast two names,
from before and after the trap, the gun,

the mower's scythe, saw's live teeth, and
come when called trailing stories like a leash—

for they are local legends, veterans of accident
about whom strangers inevitably ask

and whom men especially favor (if never coddle),
oblige with the necessary words or hand,

tail-thumping, open-window ride in their pickups,
sticks they want so very much to fetch,

and do—retrieving even thrown stones
with such uncommon ease you'd think they run

to skin and bone like some old friend
because they've learned balance

depends on lean, and less,
and seem to accept what is missing

if feeling a little hungry always.

My Friend Said

"It's always the same rat," speaking of
the rat he, when a boy, watched emerge
out the city sewer grate
like mythic Eurydice from Hades:

the same rat, he said, that appeared
beside his car's right front tire 40 years later
in his garage in rural Vermont.

Perhaps the same rat I poisoned
when she or he took to gnawing the house,
teeth tap-tapping within my cellar wall
like some sorry Fortunato—

though, I acknowledge, it is hard to drum up
much sympathy for them:
like the murine multitudes I watched

a yellow-jacketed City crew bash and shovel
into their idling sanitation trucks,
rodent blood staining
the block's concrete sidewalk

like shadows not quite bleached clean—
sidewalk I could never look at again
without thinking of Hiroshima.

Dead Frogs

People of a certain age
might remember junior high school
biology class, the labs and
formaldehyde-pickled frogs
sort of swimming crammed in glass
jars bulk-purchased
for us to learn something.
Though I recall little
except that embalmer's smell
and how my frog lay
on the dissecting tray flat on its back,
waiting to be opened.
And how most of the guys acted
as if death were a joke,
sought to gross out
with frog innards, stolen
ocular marbles.

I suspect many of them
had already done their share
of damage, harmed
various frogs, turtles,
snakes, newts, for boys will be
boys (not to mention girls),
and we were young.
Back then few thought much
about what was happening
outside, like the summer when
bullfrogs ceased thrumming,
mouths and marsh plugged
with trucked gravel.
Or when, like angels
heralding spring, the peepers
no longer sang.

In the photograph I look at,
some of the world's last
southern mountain
yellow-legged frogs float flat
on their backs, slack thighs
mocking any pretense at jumping,
pallid bellies and throats
marbled with blue-green rot.
Like a killing field's corpses
they clutter the stream.
Which is not to trivialize humans
or frogs, these dead
whose mouths gape skyward, opened
as if on the cusp of being
kissed, the spell that is death—
the spell that is us—
    broken.

Driving Through the Reservation

I think of the dogs also
                cut down like children
at the entrance to houses and kivas
because they objected
                to the slaughter of innocents,
to the bullets like arrows and Anglos
caught up in the free-for-all
                massacre of sheep, cattle,
horses, goats—livestock
Uncle Sam declared too much in 1934;
                  and I picture the carcasses
left to rot among the scrub brush
and prickly pears, the collapsed dumb
                animals in heaps
like the mounds of bison,
(over 30 million slain in twenty years);
                like the Sioux fallen
at Little Big Horn, the painted Lakota,
Cheyenne, Arapaho warriors
                whose bodies also
were forbidden the natives to touch
or bury their bones;
            and I hear the blue sky crack
with the cries of Navaho
children, women, men as they looked on
                the flat table
of the plains and gouged arroyos, sandstone
cliffs like ladders leading toward
                the mute ancestral gods—
and I imagine
only dark birds move:
            ravens at the feast.

Impressions

One hopes for barrel, cereus, organ pipe cactus,
thick Saguaro arms raised
in praise, or supplication, above the desert floor;

this far north, only aloe, clumps
of green prickly pears' needled paddles
spotted with flowers like rugosa roses
yellow, pink, white, orange
brighten sand.

We pass the first of the casinos,
dull as any Dollar Store—
walls of corrugated tin, flat roof, gravel lot
where magic marker signs shout sales
of a sort—
    "WIN BIG!
$10,000 JACKPOT!!"—
words to pull the locals in,
the usual tourist gamblers,
the curious, the bored,
the simply hot.

Farther on, the plains spread out like cloth
stitched with tufts of sheep,
goats, horses,
trailer shacks like cardboard boxes
littering sand-lot yards, no grass
green as our paper-money presidents;

here and there, cottonwoods stand,
tied dogs drowse
in shallow pools of shade.

Later, we stop for dinosaurs:
marvel at Mesozoic footprints signing

this land's once-wet page,
think of children's finger-painted hands,
Hollywood Boulevard.

The Natives run the show:

Grandmother tells of palaeosaur and stegosaur,
of the men who came to verify;
on the side her daughter sells
silver rings, beads hand-strung,
ubiquitous turquoise.

She shows us stones
she claims are unhatched eggs:
and we choose to believe.

The Joshua Trees

The Joshua trees
raise their jazzy arms skyward
as if to praise, sing

hallelujah: thus
the Mormon settlers perceived
spiny succulents

that guided Brigham
on toward Zion's Great Salt Lake.
But now like martyrs

the Joshua trees
blaze in the hot Mohave
desert, place of rock

and sand, kangaroo
rats, pocket mice, tortoise, bats,
conspicuously

sun-basking lizards,
among too many others
to describe or name.

The Joshua trees
burn, flare like old-time prophets'
torches lighting us

to nowhere. No tree
or bush, no Cholla cactus
speaks inside its flames,

ineffably de-
claims with fire's tongue "I Am"—
Jehovah gone dumb

as the stars above
this latest conflagration
of trees, of what lives

within or under.
The Joshua trees burn, black-
ening to pillars

of char and ashen
arms raised—until the whirlwind
blows the desert clean.

Saguaro Reverie

> "Enormous nude green hairless tubes with arms
> That look like prehistory reaching out without hands."
> —Frederick Seidel, "Surf's Up,"

People prone to whimsy dress them
in cowboy hats, gingham aprons,
ho-ho crimson suits—
though they're as far from Santa
as any armadillo.

Some gun-toting buckaroos
used to shoot them
for practice, fun, out of boredom;
not coincidentally,
we label cactus parts as "bodies,"
"skin," "skeletons," "arms"—

Fact: In Arizona it is a felony to kill
    or kidnap one.
Fact: It can take them ten years
    to grow one inch.

I tend to see them as handless
supplicants reaching
toward their barbed god, Grand-
Father of desert cactus
and succulents, whose spiky viridescence
the wise do not embrace.

And yet...
I have dreamt prickly legions
hovering over the Sonoran sands—
dreamed green invasions,
their pleated columns
singing to the moon.

Hey Diddle . . .

Atop the steel communications tower
above the local bottle
redemption center, ospreys
are building a nest.

Watching one soar trailing strings
of vine, I think
of a child's kite freely surfing the wind.

Hour after hour
the male raptor wings
through air to earth to pillar
then back again, delivers picked up sticks
and scraps of green
to his architecturally-inclined mate,
who decides where
to place them for their avian installation.

Day after day
the nest grows higher, rounder.
Eggs and Easter bonnets,
jagged top hats upended occupy my mind
as steel and sticks, satellite and bird,
dish and bowl conjoin
under the swollen moon.

Surely somewhere a little dog laughs.

Another Dog Story

My dog, too, killed them, brought home not just one wing
but the entire bird: I recall exiting the yellow bus
to race up the hill, hoping to get there before
my mom got home—

how sometimes there was nothing but the dog, wagging
as if to say, "See, I've been a good boy,"
and sometimes there was a riot of feathers
strewn over our yard.

And I'd grab the shovel from the shed to bury the bird
near the willow, hope the dog, who'd never deigned
to chase a single ball, wouldn't of a sudden
convert to golden retriever.

For days after I'd pray we wouldn't be found out:
because Butch was my dog, and my mom had said,
"One more time, that dog goes to the pound"—
no matter how I pleaded

it wasn't his fault, he just couldn't resist the flurried flapdoodle
of the chase. So I reasoned, just as I tried to tell myself
the chickens were no different than the mice
her cat laid like temple offerings

on our back stoop. (Though I knew better, knew from the first
slack cluckless carcass.) And sometimes I dreamed
their bones sprouting from our yard
like pale fingers to accuse:

nightmares I could never tell my mother were about chickens
I had buried to save Butch, whom I loved—and who,
one Saturday morning, at last managed
to catch the left-front tire

of the Sealtest milk and eggs delivery truck.

Free Range

> "Americans expected to eat 1.45 billion chicken wings on SuperBowl Sunday." — *National Chicken Council, 2024*

This snowless winter the flock wanders the grove
pecking among spent flora, deliberate
as accountants. Feathers fluffed

against the cold, they suggest intrepid explorers
snug within their Arctic puffer parkas.
The sky does not fall on them,

nor fox or man disquiet
where three-toed feet step, delicate
as ballerinas who dance *en pointe*—

then of a sudden rake sequestered insect, tick
the chickens pluck to picnic on.
Sun-bespotted, their colors resonate:

russet, chestnut, olive- and midnight-black,
white-speckled Plymouth rock gray, crimson
combs bobbing among the brush.

This super-cold Sunday I watch as hens wander
freely, alive among the stripped trees
and leaves' scratched eruptions.

The Ladies in Their Hats

The ladies in their hats
are women of privilege and wealth,
as their dresses—garnished with lace,
beads, pearls, fine embroidery—
attest. Likewise, their hats:
marvelous confections of cloth, wire,
feathers, even entire birds
posed amid twigs, leaves, nests, eggs:
wondrous, perched or sitting,

wings stretched as if in flight.
Also long since dead, the ladies
in their photographs sepia-tinged
stare beneath the brims and
severed wings of Everglades herons,
wood storks, ibises, roseate
spoonbills; mute testimony
to how fortunate they are, they were,

to have lived in such an age
when feathers were all the rage.
And oh, the beauty of
the snowy egrets—the white gossamer
of their prized nuptial barbs
worth twice the price of gold,
ethereal as a dream of angels

or dandelion fluff: so airy,
the ladies seem almost to levitate
(a paradox of sorts) beneath.
Nor are they discomfited by egrets—
shot, scalped, stripped
like common leghorn chickens—

that clutter the Floridian waters
where men walk round island rookeries
on birds' sodden stepping stones,
birds good now only to feed the fish
and gators' grinning logs.

While elsewhere in staged dioramas
in the museums of natural history,
more *avifauna* brood, stilled-lives all,
as the ladies in their hats

smile from within thick family albums
and wrought silver frames
that grace nightstands, shelves, mantles—

smile, as the photographer instructed,
thumb poised to shoot.

Fake Birds

"You know they're not real," he says
when I point to the finches at the
feeder, their small bodies turning
from drab olive green to buttercup
gold—surely a sign of spring.

"They're fake birds," he says.
"Used to spy on us. And that gang
of starlings perched on the power
line? Also surveillance drones. Just
look at how they're watching us while
they sap the line's energy."

I try to joke, birdwatchers watch
birds—why not the reverse?

"You don't get it," he says. "The
government's been spying on us for
decades, ever since the '90s when
the CIA killed off the real birds with
a strain of avian flu engineered to
dissolve their bodies."

"All birds?" I ask. "Sparrows? Owls?
Chickens?"

"Chickens? Shit! Have you ever looked
into a chicken's eyes? And don't even
get me started on owls!"

"Pet cockatiels? Toucans, parrots?
My aunt's blue budgie?"

"What better plant?" he says. "Right inside
our very homes."

"You can not be serious," I say.

"Don't you get it? That's what they're counting on—it's so absurd they think no one will believe it. When you think about it, it's brilliant!"

"So they just watch us?"

"Mostly they spy, record, though some, like vultures and crows, are cleaners— not just roadkill, but bodies they want 'disappeared.' Hummers, woodpeckers, act as assassins—don't have those sharp beaks for nothing! Storks, too. Their bills can pummel you to mush in minutes."

"But I watch them eat, I see their eggs ..."

"No," he says. "You just think you do. It's all a trick of perception and expectations. And while we're on the subject, I have my doubts whether earthworms are real."

"Bird nests?"

"Made by children in Vietnam and installed by federal agents overnight. Along with 'eggs' that sometimes are incendiary devices."

"Feathers?" I ask. "Left on the ground?"

"Taken off some real birds before they died and from specimens in natural history museums. Occasionally a drone will scatter a few to augment the lie."

"Birdsong?"

"Recordings played on a loop."

"Bird poop?"

"A tracking device for when you're in places like the city where there aren't a lot of birds."

"What about pigeons?" I ask.

"Ah," he sighs. "The real pigeons survived. They always do. But everyone knows that pigeons lie."

To Neuter, or Not

They're at it again, fighting or fucking—
an eternal din
              of feline decibels
rending the dark
as if Bosch's infernal harp
played outside our door.
                      How they yowl,
having at it! Hard to imagine
our own sweet kitty
among that caterwauling clowder:
                    Tom,
who, yesterday, lay curled
on my lap, celestially
purring—
            my bewhiskered Mister
Hyde, now gone
to join the rumpus,
                  Bedlam so loud
the stars shiver, the moon
stuffs its ears
with tufts of cloud—
              'til at last
our prodigal
puss drags home,
half drowned in the well

Falling Iguanas

Another cold snap,
another Falling Iguanas Alert:

Best not to be out and about or,
under a somber palm, gaze
long at the moon illuming the eternal waves
when temperatures plummet,
rigid lizards rain.

Rain from magnolia and cypress,
thatch, palmetto, palm—
rain like cats and dogs or Old Testament
plague: plague of iguanas arboreal
Miami has set a bounty on (so it's said)
amid citizen demands for
"iguana remediation,"

while certain locals try to develop
a taste for gallina de palo,
"chicken of the tree," as the cold
creatures' heavy fruits plop:

showers of benumbed lizards
clogging the drains,
splotching sidewalks and parking lots;
denting Teslas, Audis, Hondas,
as if God Themselves had dropped a clutch
of odd rocks from the overpass.

Or, upon Floridian emerald lawns and
paradisal sands, set a bevy
of the immobilized,
these reptiles that might have slipped—
like Alice into Wonderland's

painted roses and flamingo mallets—
from the pen of Lewis Carroll;

iguanas fallen, waiting
on the dawn: on the sun that,
like a warm prince,
will kiss them into waking.

Like the Cheese, the Camel

Like the cheese, the camel stands alone
knee-deep in pasture, pollen-golden

and fluttering Cleopatra lashes, timeless as
its namesake mountain, Camel's Hump:

vision implausible here,
where our Green Mountains governor banned

elephants like some others would ban illegal aliens.

Though, at first, one likely does not perceive
camel nor outlawed pachyderm;

sees—there, beyond the oblivious Holsteins grazing—
almost anything other: some trick of light

and shadow, a mote's misshapen cow,
or (oh rare annunciation!)

moose antlerless cropping daisies.

Summer, when camel materializes from mist
like a dream of sand and sphinx,

one thinks Arabia, Lawrence of—
recalls racing ruminants and caravans

of yellow buses shuttling to the zoo
children who'll queue for popsicles, cotton candy,

a chance to see the salt-and-pepper pandas,
tigers, monkeys, bears, one sage gorilla

pondering single-channel television;

as, beyond all big-name attractions,
the few dromedaries pose as if carved

or stamped on a pack of smokes, impervious
to those who scurry past,

sticky hands trailing an oasis of balloons
all the way to Pennsylvania Avenue.

While in Vermont the lone camel

stands knee-deep in grass and flowers wild,
dew-glazed dome crowned by the sun

as if to remind that beauty
incongruous often is.

La Brea Tar Pits

One imagines some mastodon
up to its Pleistocene knees in tar,
sinking deeper in crude
bitumen, suction like quicksand
        smothering
until only the trunk remains,
periscope up
as if to grasp the last
breath of air.
      But, one learns, not
such L.A. melodrama as that:
more like a mouse
stuck to an adhesive trap
trying to tear
        its tiny pink feet off
the tacky strip before
it starves.
   No doubt
La Brea's pits looked safe enough,
despite any methane
bubbling pitch like black pudding
on the range—
        thus, mastodon
and mammoth, ground sloth,
giant bison, camel
and short-faced bear stepped . . .
enmired paws/
        hooves/
            feet:
a glacial age menagerie
soon enough encased
in asphalt
(not unlike those mosquitoes
one sees shut inside
        resin's pretty amber).

Add to this glutinous mix
dire wolves by the hundreds,
a clowder of saber-
toothed cats—
              all sucked in
by visions of prey for the taking,
the promise of
easy pickings from
La Brea's viscous platter:
            easy as shooting
fish in a barrel.
Barrel, one might say,
both predator and prey
    were over,
stuck on the crust
of seeping petroleum, and sinking
slowly in
the tarry darkness
    of the future—
the future now
that is ours.

Where Balloons Go

They are releasing balloons
to honor the old, the new, the dead,
or, as likely, the living
survivors of our latest horror,
if not those elders who yet linger
like the endangered sea turtles, pelicans.

Perhaps they are releasing balloons
to celebrate this or that
festive occasion: gender-reveal,
birthday, wedding,
Walmart opening.

Watching that helium lift-off
of swollen heads trailing natal strings,
I imagine stillborns
soaring heavenward to God;
recall deft hands forming
faceless dogs, tigers, giraffes—
hear the plaints of latex
being twisted, see the bodies plumped
that too soon deflated.

Recall again the grasped string
of a leashed friend
tugging to be free—
that sudden ascension into the ether—
the first of losses grieved.
And how the child was lessoned,
everything that rises falls.

Think of Penguins

Antarctica fractured—
"nothing we can do but watch
the sea rise," scientists say.

Think of penguins.
Think, though we'll be long since gone,
how much we'll miss them:
miss their Charlie Chaplin wobble
and avian perseverance
so heroic, so absurd.

Think of loss
that should be inconceivable
as death to a child.
Think of family and friends borne away
on death's cold tide.

Picture a man laid out in tuxedo and tie
as if sleeping, as if he might
at any moment rise
from the white tufted satin;
and how he looks
less a man than an Emperor
penguin laid on its back in the coffin
that itself seems like a canoe
adrift among the pale lilies
and chrysanthemums.
Recall the inscription,
"Gone but Not Forgotten."

Think of things torn, dropped, broken;
shattered like grandmothers'
crystal or fine china
we carelessly let slip through our hands.
Think of the people;

but also the tusked elephants
trumpeting apocalypse
and whales whose timbers litter the sea floor

and the funny suckered feet
of small Amazonian frogs
and the wild tigers
that once striped the dark.

Think again of penguins,
of those flightless birds who stand
at the world's shrinking rim.
Think of the pale zeroes of their eggs
and the unborn inside
and the eggs that have cracked
or simply frozen.

Think of the ones
who incubate the duds.
Wonder how long it takes them to know.

Champlain Polar Bears

Why their imprudent desire
to enter the water
cold as January? So cold

the lake has to be broken, a locked door
behind which fish drowse suspended
while people soldier in,

doughty souls unheeding those
who stand ankle-deep
as if to ponder how their life

has come to this
precise Arctic moment . . .

then immerse belly-first,
sea lions sliding
from the ledge of common sense.

None linger long
nor plumb the tenebrous depths.

In then out,
they quit Champlain's frigid font
for humdrum towels,

cups of steam,
the stand-by ER crew.

If asked, they say this is what it means
to live on the sensate edge:
shiver, seize the day.
And for a few lunatic moments,
they seem fantastical
as the bears elsewhere;

though they are plainly human,
who neither cling to ice
nor swim the widening leagues between.
Nor do they drown.

Storm Warnings

"And what rough beast, its hour come round at last,
Slouches toward Bethlehem to be born?"
—*William Butler Yeats, "The Second Coming"*

Torn from their pasture moorings, the cows move downstream.
One thinks of New Orleans, of the rivers of the streets
and propane tanks like strange sea creatures
drifting, finless, leaking.

Of wagging roof-top dogs and the men who rowed past
floating leagues of wood and paper, shit and plastic.
And the people who chose to stay
or who were left behind,
people impotent as Noah's neighbors pleading "Save Us,"
anger like a three-days corpse
risen on the oily rainbow surface of their loss.

Only, this is Vermont (land of green mountains,
100% pure maple syrup, Ben & Jerry's):
now battered by the blowhard bully
we could not stop
nor lift one finger to stop the heartbreak
of the lost farms and houses
and covered bridges that were so picturesque
and so apocalyptic going under,
the same as our neighbor and his son
swept into wet oblivion.

Katrina... Irene... Sandy...
A Jersey behemoth buckles,
boardwalk roller-coaster up to its flanks in water,
in the tide that is rising.
Harvey... Irma... Maria... Florence...

One thinks of omens and Holsteins,
the Second Coming. Of rough beasts bawling
like drowning saxophones.

Used to Be

I'd worry
not especially
about the mushroom cloud
I pictured erupting
near the riderless seesaws
and wind-crazed swings—
worried instead whether
my blob of bubble gum,
pink as raw meat,
would stay stuck under
the desk I crouched beneath,
while the big clock
on the cinderblock wall
ticked toward doom . . .
until All-Clear rang.

Funny,
to feel nostalgic
about those civil defense drills
now, now
when assault rifles
rend children unrecognizable
as fresh road kill
and no one, not even teacher,
gets to raise a hand
to ask to leave the classroom
where bullets rain
blood and brains
as sirens scream like mothers,
like struck children,
and *shelter in place*
means forever.

What I Remember:

1. The makeshift chapel
   in the house down the road,
   home to grief

2. The gull-gray coffin
   that sat like a boat
   stranded on a shoal
   of chrysanthemums and lilies

3. The lone wreath
   that whispered "Rest in Peace"

4. The stilled body
   that lay sunken on quilted satin
   the color of old lace

5. The pain-etched face
   masking the woman
   we called mother

6. The uninvited guest
   who strode,
   young child in tow,
   all the way to the waiting coffin

7. Those words:
   "See, that's what Death looks like."

Mary

Mary the elephant hangs in the air

by the steel chain wound round her neck

and hoisted up by the railroad crane

brought in especially for the occasion.

Slowly she swings above,

slowly she strangles as a few dogs sniff the feet

of the crowd that gawks below:

the old and young men and women,

the babies snug in dreams of milk and cotton,

the clusters of bug-eyed children.

In Erwin, Tennessee, it is the prime of lynching

and such reality shows of another century

no doubt more wrenching than Mary's

or the man she crushed in the traveling circus

where she entertained the multitudes.

As she does now—her public

execution, that crowd of 2500 souls

grasping picnic hampers packed with pork

and pie despite the September drizzle,

while Mary above performs

like some extraordinary high wire acrobat:

a trouper to the last

gasp of her body's deflating balloon.

In Tennessee, it is the Year of Our Lord 1916.

Soon boys will take off to join the show

where some will die beside the bloated

bodies of horses, men and mules;

some, caught in the wire's barbed embrace,

will pray to Our Lady of Sorrows for mercy

and probably receive none.

They may have time before the canvas drops

to think of mothers and fathers,

of sweethearts waiting who will marry others.

Of favorite fishing holes, best dogs.

Of being children once.

The sky above will be gray as lead;

looking up, they may remember

Mary's pendulum.

Frost:

The elephant
ears wither, cold-
singed leaves
large as Thanks-
giving platters if not
ears of pachyderms:

Save for the young
clumsy Dumbos
nuzzling mothers'
felled trees, mothers
blind men only see
as ivory tusks
(like parings
of the moon)—

and blood
that stains the earth
the same as spring
rains after drought
when baobabs blossom
and elephants fly
inside the bellies
of birds.

My Neighbor's Pigs

My neighbor's pigs snuff indelicately.
The pigs number three,
same as in the classic tale of,
if no longer little,
still fattening toward their fate.

Lacking straw, sticks or brick,
the pigs dwell on earth beneath a sheet-
metal roof inside a wire fence
just on the other side
of my neighbor's tree line.

The Wolf (Big, Bad) is my neighbor
who routinely explodes
in curses as he Looney-Tunes rages
over some offense
that rarely has to do with
his porcine innocents,
and everything to do with
his free-range clucks
Br'er Fox/Raccoon/Possum/Skunk/Coyote
hopefully eye.

The pigs have no names like Wilbur,
Peppa, Porky, Piglet, Bernice,
Babe, Miss Piggy,
Napoleon...
                Anonymity
being, I suppose, preferred
when one entertains
visions of ham and Christmas
sausage, bacon, chops:
the next incarnation of Eleusinian swine
sizzling in the pan.

Taking the dogs out,
I breathe the stink of my neighbor's pigs,
fetid as a swamp at low tide:
my dogs wag, happily
inhale the malodorous bouquet.

Beneath the waxing moon
we listen to the pigs
snore in apnean fits and starts
as if troubled by unpleasant dreams.

Doesn't Much Matter

*The bullfighters frequently cut the bull's spinal cord
with a dagger to make his death more visually appealing
to the spectators. His ears and tail are then cut off.*

Suppose it doesn't much matter
when refugees like lemmings take to the sea

and camel-less caravans face a wall
of government razor wire
and the latest round

of fly-spotted
pot-bellied
children

intrudes upon the screen
the same as the many rheumy-eyed kittens

and quivering corner-crouching dogs
just when we're about to watch the game.

And the glaciers are melting,
the oceans rising,
bees dying,
trees dying,
gorilla,
elephant,
orangutan—

name after name crossed off the list—
our very own children

mown down
while attending civics class

or finger painting
smiley suns—

almost anything you can imagine
on the decline, including basic civility,

mutual R-E-S-P-E-C-T.

So what difference does it make
if 250,000 bulls die each year in the ring?

250,000 methane machines
skewered in service to the oldest drama

of all: man facing death,
man wielding death's dagger—

that visual coup de gras
Hemingway so loved, lusted after

(somewhat like Pasiphae,
who, so to speak, took the bull by his horns).

It's culture,
it's entertainment,
it's heavy
real-life symbolism:

toro picador-pierced, fallen on its knees
as if in prayer, as if

offering its body up to the matador,
he the "slayer of bulls,"

as the crowd roars, ecstatic
petals raining down
on his blood

red *muleta*,
on man and bull,
one dumb "Wooly Bully"

among the many sprouting spears,
a dying pinata

whose carcass soon will be dragged
off to the local abattoir;

where, I suppose, everything goes
after the show has ended,
no B.S.—
refugees and dogs,
gorillas and kittens,
elephants,
orangutans,
children,
bees . . .

"Ole!" applauding throng
in all its Pamplona lather—
not unlike when we watch Ravens
vs. 'skins football

because we think this much matters.

No Poetry Lies

No poetry lies
in the lucent rainbow sheen
of the sea's oiled skin;
nor in the birds—
    gull, curlew,
gannet, tern,
    pelican, plover,
booby, auk,
    goose, duck,
    egret, swan,
cormorant—
who, like children
after the big yellow bus
has skidded off the road,
cannot comprehend why
their wings will not work.

No poetry lies
in the moon-faced sea cattle
our boats incise;
nor in the whales—
    gray, right,
bowhead, minke,
    sperm, humpback,
orca, beluga,
porpoise, pilot,
    killer, dolphin,
bottlenose—
the last blue titans,
whose bones like broken cathedrals
marble the depths
or litter the shore the same
as our tide-borne trash.

It is best to remember
neither the sea
nor the birds
nor the manatees
nor the whales
care whether we ache for them.

Nor are they poems
to be read on a Sunday,
as quickly forgotten
as yesterday's news.

Nor will they grieve for us
as we walk off
the edge of the world.

1968

All that day our flag climbed up and down the pole
as if a ship were foundering.
People cried, cursed, rioted.
That night, some students threw a party to celebrate,
while we sat in the dorm glued to the TV
and watched cities blaze.
Sunday a group of us attended services
at the Holy Redeemer Baptist Church
on the far edge of town.
Were we welcome?
I do not recall.
I believe they tolerated with grace our naivety.

Later that week I drove through Baltimore
past burnt-out blocks, glass-strewn
sidewalks where pigeons walked, iridescent
among the shards—
everywhere the smell of tear gas and char,
the city strange as Beirut or Saigon.

The Tet Offensive,
My Lai,
MLK's assassination,
a drafted friend boxed home,
the three months it took my mother to die—
it was a bad year all around.
As Bobby's funeral train wound from L.A. to D.C.,
I threw out my campaign buttons,
bumper stickers, belief;
people stood along the tracks, waving
scraps of the red, white and blue,
while on a different channel jungles flamed,
birds and tigers gone to ash.
All around, a bad year,
and only early June.

I remember driving home
in Bay fog like a pall: it seemed everywhere
history was being born.
Yet I could barely see the road.

The Dog in *Life*

I like the United States of America,
I like the way we all live without fear.
I like to vote for my choice, speak my mind, raise my voice,
Yes, I like it here.

The dog in *Life* magazine could be my neighbor's
German Shepherd Laika,
except she isn't

running to greet me or playing fetch,
but instead strains at her leash,
jaws open, sharp white

cuspids about to clamp down on
the arm of the boy, the boy
who could be my own

school mate but isn't,
can not be,
because Anne Arundel County

has not yet worked out the details
of Supreme Court-mandated
desegregation;

while my mother declares she won't teach
"any pigtail pickaninny"
and Uncle Vernon fumes,

clicks off the news, says he's glad
he'll be dead and
buried when all this "civil rights shit

hits the fan."
Which is about the time
I begin to see the people I love

aren't quite who I thought
they were—
though not to be counted

among those frozen in mid-spit
in *Life*'s black and white
photographs

or rabidly cheering
a few years later at the rally
for George Wallace,

whom they wanted to be President
of *their* America:
the America, I was starting to realize,

that was mine also,
and didn't have so much in common
with what I'd been taught;

like those morning songs
we sang before class began,
and that I hear still,

marveling
at what I took for granted then.
Though anyone can see

even now
the dog in *Life*
bites.

Synchronicity

"The only reason for time is so that everything doesn't happen at once."
—Albert Einstein

"Doomsday Clock Set at 100 Seconds to Midnight"
—NBC, January 23, 2020

This morning the Kit-Cat Klock®
fell from my kitchen wall, hit the floor
as if a bomb had blown
the classic clock to smithereens,
                    googly eyeballs
scattering like panicked mice,
AA battery headed for the dark place
beneath the refrigerator.

I went about retrieving the remains:
black and white plastic cat's
tuxedoed body,
chest inscribed 1 through 12;
stilled pendulum tail,
                that Cheshire face
cracked like an egg.
The incident occurred just as I
was about to break
the morning egg and trying
not to think everything,
                like my CT scan,
depended on how I cracked it—
quick and clean,
with the one-handed finesse
of a five-star chef,
              no shards of shell

specking the yolk or albumen
for me to fish out,
no drop of my blood staining
what fries in the non-stick pan.
                    But then the clock
fell—
which set me
to thinking about Time
both slow and fast, long and brief,
and how much of it we spend
simply,
    or not so simply,
waiting:
at the market,
at the airport,
at the car wash
and drive-through;
on the phone while we listen
to a disembodied voice tell us that
we must "Wait."
                Wait
among the philodendrons
and ficus trees in the reception lobbies
and fluorescent examining rooms
of dentists, doctors,
specialists . . .
           Wait
for the friend
who said she'd pick us up
at half past ten,
who herself is waiting
for the light to change.
                Wait,
as we did in school
in our classrooms
while the minutes passed like years
as we watched

the hands of the big wall clock
spasm toward 12 - - -
                       the bell to ring.

As I do now, waiting
for something
to begin,
    something
to end.

Visitation

I assume he came in the night or just at dusk
when I wasn't looking.
I picture him lurking in the copse, waiting.
I see the coarse dark fur;
paws large as boys' baseball mitts;
the essential claws, teeth.

Ticks stud his ears and snout,
woodland jewelry.
I imagine him as young, adolescent,
with much yet to learn.

It's the seed he's after, black-oil sunflower,
and suet caged inside the feeders
that, despite the warnings,
I've hung on the crooks of the poles
like lit lanterns.

When he ventures forth, not wrath but desire
turns welded iron to saplings
he bows toward the earth:
the heavens rain gold
suet, seed, feeders.

This morning, standing among the ruins
I think of Viking raiders.
But also of Gabriel, the archangel
of annunciations.

Among the cloisters of the trees,
the birds sing like monks.

Speaking of Fat Bear Week, Katmai, Alaska

—Bears lurk on the edge of waking.

There, bears bigger than pianos
and certain cars wade
in the Falls, jaws opened wide
to welcome in leaping fish, feast
upon silver salmon

as people online vote for the fattest
bear, one who will wear
the crown for a year, perhaps
avoid our *slings and arrows*.

Elsewhere, brown bears dunk
in pools to escape dog-days heat
then emerge, shaggy hair
streaming waterfalls
above flung peanuts, Cracker Jacks,

while behind the zoo's viewing glass
polar twins swim,
pale fur sparking as if on fire,
trailing embers through turquoise water.

Here, I watch one burly bruin
dismantle my compost's wormy layers
to fastidiously savor
dogs' stale kibble, smatterings
of blue, of red berries,

before he ambles into the dusk
like something dreamed,
woodland phantasm
imagined more than seen.

This morning, I awake to rived hives,
emptied bird feeders'
iron crooks bowed toward earth
like broken question marks—
and *BEAR* the answer.

November

Looking out the living room window
I see in the garden doves
ambulate like ladies promenading
in the park of another century,
perhaps Seurat's—although the doves
carry no parasols…

In the stone bowl
water lies shut behind its skin,
frost gilds the asters
gone to seed…

Wind-whipped oaks rattle,
the flock whirrs up
in a gust of wings…

All day their mourning calls linger
as, in the last flower's
gold center,
a cold bee clings
to yesterday.

Ode: Ice Grips

On the kitchen floor, cold tears
streak faux brick vinyl where the pair lies,
shucked:
    Incurved cat's-cradles
of rubber and wire sequined with ice,
curled toward themselves
like caterpillars of a sudden touched
        or crescent
horns taken from some Himalayan
hirsute bull about to gong,
bellow, awaken snow
        into avalanche: Imagine
being blotted thusly,
no tracks to mark the spot
where you went under,
        drowned in the white
cascade like a lake-dumped witch
too late averred innocent—
who wouldn't confess,
        seeing that silver filigree
coil round its black worm
like some eerie thing that smacks
of the medieval, crafted
    to torture one's sole?
Why, even the prince would
struggle to slip
on Cinderella's exquisite foot
        the recalcitrant grip,
this elastic, hands strain to stretch.
Transformation waits
upon metallic teeth:
        Again I, sure-footed
Tibetan yak, tread the rink
of the yard as my Vermont dogs slide,
four-legged pucks.

Off-Hours at the Launderette

One waits:

Contemplates if not the world
or the wall-mounted television's blank
Cyclopean eye—
if not *People* or *Good Housekeeping*,
Rutland Herald newspaper
or leaflets proclaiming *"He Is Risen!"*—
not the dollar-&-coin dispenser
or yellow plastic bucket-
seat chairs

Then perhaps
the absence of others,
whether texting or talking
to cellular ghosts, phones
pressed like seashells to ears
as children shriek down
and up the aisles
of washers, dryers, folding
tables, bump and crash laundry
carts as if at a Six Flags
escape

Or perhaps
one simply watches
from her side of the dryer

    sheets

pillowcases
                   towels

       blouses
shirts

  socks

    jeans
               panties
                                 bras

tumble and spin,
caught up in the centripetal motion
of forced-air heat

Watches as the once-sodden
clumps of cloth whirl
like Toto and Dorothy, cow and house
inside the dryer's hot tornado
while one snagged zipper
rat-tat-tats
and the second load sloshes,
someone's heavy toddler
at play in the tub.

Aquarium

No dolphins schooled to be obedient as dogs here:

Just this colossal tank where glaucous turtles glide,

slow as sloths. Sharks, too, and eels,

multitudes of fish—sun, clown, puffer,

butterfly, parrot, pilot—

a fleet of rays, sting and manta,

adrift on silken, languid wings.

Here even the stars are alive.

And angels rainbow-hued

and wee steeds that swim, exquisite.

Here, jellyfish pulse like hearts:

plain or fringed, clear as cellophane, they seem

numinous as children waiting to be born

as they pass our faces peering in

behind the glass that weeps.

Sometimes the Trees

The hills are alive
with the momentary beauty of things
lit, going up—
      pyrotechnics
that take our breaths
away, like the smoke that stays,
shrouding the familiar.
               Stone sizzles,
brush crackles as if wax
paper, trees flame, trans-
formed to Roman candles—
             EXPLODE
like bombs in backpacks
or dropped from the sky: Atomic,
and otherwise.
 From Amazon
to Oregon, California to
Colorado, Canada to
Australia, the wildfires flare,
               scorched skies
rain Inferno, ignite
understories, the dark and
light of memory:
      that smell
of things left too long on the grill,
char and ash
limning each green soul;
      the blackened
limbs and bones of those
too slow.
This year I dream
   arboreal holocaust.
Awake to the screams
of trees.

What Remains

Behind the chain-link fence of residence
we dragged on cigarettes, lips pursed
to the kiss of addiction,
fingers tattooing knees, table,
plaster walls with an unsteady pulse.
Hard rock stuttered from the box
and we sailed on its static,
rolled with the Stones—
outside where women squeezed in plaid lawn chairs
turned sidewalk to boardwalk,
virgins leaped a swinging rope
and old men laughed, watching girls'
brown legs blur like their youth.

Mostly we stayed in,
ears plugged to the sirens
and friends calling us back
to what had got us there, in the house
where we worked or sat
in a circle of words
hurled like bottles, like bricks;
while out on the street plywood howled turf,
howled "Fast Eddie Loves Cindi 4ever,"
and dreams cost a nickel a bag
in the alleys bejeweled with the glimmer
of glass, of needles and eyes
of the rats that threaded the maze,
their piper the flung crusts of our lives
until the city's iron ball swings.

Some Things in This World

Some things in this world would break your heart
if you let them. This alone is sufficient reason
to bury the television
remote under the barberry bush
whose red tears this autumn
look more than ever like blood.
   Reason enough to shun the plague
   of amiable newscasters so eager
   to tell you where today
   and in what particular manner
   the sky has fallen.
   Reason no longer to grieve
   what has been lost
   or will be.

One desires solely to think upon the meticulous grace
of the sloths and dangling orangutans
as they move through the rain
forest that is not yet ash.
   Solely to watch these forest-dwellers
   move, languid as the moon.
   To forget the hands
   that hold the matches
   as we gape like frogs
   whose adhesive scarlet feet
   cling like the last berries
   to the bush.

Notes

"Dead Frogs," is inspired by and uses quotes from a photo caption in *National Wildlife* (February-March 2019).

"Fake Birds" is a mix of my own take upon the "conspiracy," full treatment of which can be found in *Birds Aren't Real: The True Story of Mass Avian Murder and The Largest Surveillance Campaign in US History,* by Peter McIndoe and Connor Gaydos (2024).

In "Think of Penguins," a paraphrase from *PLOS Biology* referenced in cnn.com Dec. 2022: "65% of Antarctic native species, emperor penguins top among them, will be gone by the end of the century."

"Mary": I first read of this elephant in a letter from an animal sanctuary, which included an old photo with the caption '1916 five-ton elephant lynched in TN.'

"Doesn't Much Matter," see "Bullfighting: A Spectacle of Cruelty in Three Acts," Humane Society International, 2011, www.hsi.org/news-resources/bullfighting_three_acts/.

"The Dog in *Life,*" I recall "I like the United States of America," being sung in schools in the 1950s, author unknown.

In "Synchronicity," the time quote used is often attributed to Albert Einstein, CheckYourFact.com/2019. Headline "Doomsday Clock remains at 100 seconds to midnight" from *The Bulletin of Atomic Scientists* as reported in NBC, *Forbes,* and other news sites.

In "Speaking of Fat Bear Week," the quote "Bears lurk on the edge of waking" is from an unpublished poem of mine and "slings and arrows" is borrowed from Shakespeare's *Hamlet.*

About the Author

Joyce Thomas is the author of two previous poetry collections, *Washing Birds* (Main Street Rag, 2016) and *Skins* (Fithian Press, 2001), and one nonfiction work, *Inside the Wolf's Belly: Aspects of The Fairy Tale* (Sheffield Academic Press, 1989). Her poetry has appeared in various publications, including *North American Review* and *JAMA*, as well as the anthologies *Orpheus and Company: Contemporary Poems on Greek Mythology* (UP of New England); *The Poets' Grimm: 20th Century Poems from Grimm Fairy Tales* (Story Line Press); and *Birchsong: Poetry Centered in Vermont* (Blueline Press).

Born in Annapolis, Maryland, the poet has lived in Vermont since 1980, teaching at former Castleton State College with special interests in World, English, and Children's Literature. The second Vermont State College Faculty Fellow, upon her retirement she was granted Professor Emerita status. Dr. Thomas contentedly lives in Castleton with a large dog, a small dog, a black cat, an orange cat, and a verdant cottage garden.

We Grow Our Books in Montpelier, Vermont

Learn more about our titles in Fiction, Nonfiction, Poetry and Children's Literature at the QR code below or visit www.rootstockpublishing.com.